Singled Out

Andre Vaughn

A C K N O W L E D G E M E N T S

I truly want to thank God for sending me on this much-needed vacation. The things I have learned from this experience were God ordained. I can honestly say I never lost faith or stopped believing in my God.

Next, I want to thank my wife. The way you held it down for our girls and made sure they didn't skip a beat was masterful. During our darkest hour, you decided to have my back and I truly appreciate it.

I want to give a special shout-out to my siblings. I am grateful to have you both in my life and having your support meant the world to me.

Last but not least, I thank my business partners and Bula Vita family. Normally, when a business partner goes through something like this, others turn their back on you. The love and support that all of you demonstrated helped me in ways that you never will know. We will do life together and help a lot of families, as well. Doing life together means I appreciate having you in my life and we will continue to grow together.

I am deeply grateful to all the people that I just mentioned!

Singled Out

Table of Contents

Introduction

Last year, there were 165,070 federal criminal prosecutions. Out of all of those prosecutions, 8,252 were wrongfully prosecuted. The average cost of incarceration for federal inmates is $36,299.25 per year, per inmate.

I remember my sentencing judge saying to the prosecution, "In my twenty years, she did not have a single prosecution from a bankruptcy trustee." She also said, "I just want to make sure Mr. Vaughn was not singled out." At that moment, I knew what the title of my book was going to be.

Even though I know now that this process was God-ordained, the human side of me was very disappointed that I was heading to prison. My inspiration for this book was to share with the world how you can take something very bad and turn it into a blessing. I also wanted to raise awareness about how much families go through daily.

A copy of the court transcripts and the judge’s comments are also included in this book. Writing this book taught me to never judge anyone who is going through a hardship in their own life. People have been singled out for a variety of things throughout their lives. This can cause depression, suicidal thoughts, and unhappiness.

I pray that after you have read about my journey, you will never make excuses about the things you go through in life. Always remember there is a miracle waiting for you on the other side of the mess. Keep pushing and stay positive. I found my happy place during this prison term. What the devil intended to be evil, God made good. Please share my story with everyone you know and even those whom you meet.

I have no intention of neither falsifying anything in this book nor the facts regarding my case. Instead,

I chose my family and my God over fighting against the U.S. government.

Chapter 1: In the Beginning

It all started with William Robert Vaughn and Linda Fay Compton. My parents were originally from North Carolina. They later migrated to Baltimore, got married, and my mother named herself as Linda Compton Vaughn.

My parents had three children: two boys and a girl. Before I was born, they had a miscarriage. This, I can imagine, was tragic for them, but I was grateful they never gave up. Because of their perseverance, my twin sister and I were born, Andre Lamont Vaughn and Andrea Lanae Vaughn.

My sister and I were born into this world as winners. Just think about the millions and millions of sperm we had to beat to make it to the egg. Then, we had to survive through the entire pregnancy. That is why I feel that all people are winners. If people would just tap into their greatness, they would see so much success.

It is imperative that we send our children the right messages – especially before the age of four years old. What normally happens is that our society has become lax and does not protect our childhood anymore. There are certain things that children should not be exposed to in the early stages of growth. I remember growing up and just being able to enjoy being a kid. My siblings and I stayed active and were heavily involved in athletics.

My older brother Lenard was a blessing in my life. He taught us what to do and what not to do. The three of us together had an immense sibling love. I can't even describe how my relationship with my siblings shaped my career and my life. When you have a great family foundation, you become unstoppable!

My parents created this family culture, giving us the confidence to do anything we set our minds to do. My father was the disciplinarian growing up, and my mother provided the perfect balance. With both of their support, I grew up knowing that losing was not an option. My siblings and I were competitive with everything we did. Some people have mixed views on this philosophy, but I thrived under their guidance.

My dad made sure that all of us excelled in everything we did, while my mother worked hard to be the perfect example for us growing up. I thank God every day for their guidance when I was young, and throughout my entire life. My mother always knew the right lesson to teach at exactly the right time. Every day I work hard to make her proud.

My parents both worked hard, but never really settled on a job. Their dream was to own a business. Through their struggle, I learned from them without even knowing what was happening. I remember their long meetings in the dining room when I was growing up. This taught me that just having a job was not enough: to work hard at owning something and take pride in having a true career brought happiness and fulfillment.

The biggest mistake I think we make as adults is to speak negatively to our children.

The term "money doesn't grow on trees" is quite incorrect when you think about it. Money comes from paper,

paper comes from wood, and wood comes from trees. So, actually, money does come from trees. I remember sitting at a young age just dreaming about being wealthy. It was a permanent thought that continued throughout my life.

We have to start speaking life into our children!

I have mastered using energy to achieve greatness in life. 'What is greatness', you may ask. To me, greatness is when you clearly know and understand your purpose and excel at it, too.

My family always had leadership positions in everything we did. That was non-negotiable. Creating that family culture is essential. Then once you create it, you can duplicate it with your children and your children's children. That's how a legacy is created. Now, don't think if your family foundation was not solid that you don't have a shot at success. You just have to decide to start with yourself and create a family culture that you desire.

The one thing that my parents got right was keeping my siblings and I active in all types of activities. Whether it was social, spiritual, athletic, academic, or family stuff, we were there to participate.

The beginning of any family, business, relationship, or walk with God, is the most important part. You need to start on the right foot. When you first meet someone, they should walk away and be thinking to themselves, 'Who was that'? That's when you know you have left a lasting impression on them so that they will never forget you.

It is important to be a thermostat – not a thermometer. See, the thermometer goes along to get along. The thermostat sets the tone and temperature to any and everything you do.

Your mindset plays an important part in your success in life. People don't realize that you can attract any result you desire. Most people talk about the things they either don't like or don't want, then wonder why they constantly show up in their lives over and over again. You have to be in the driver's seat of your life.

Earlier, I mentioned that my family was extremely competitive growing up. I remember people looking at it as if it was a bad thing. I really think that was one of the biggest assets because we all learned how to transfer that to the business world.

When you decide to do something great, make sure to pray about it first. Then assemble a team of people that are better than you and support them throughout the journey. I love not being the smartest person in the room. You have to be secure with your abilities and put people around you that will hide your weaknesses.

Most people have major insecurities within themselves. I used to hate when people of power had major insecurities because it affected their leadership in obvious ways. I always love creating opportunities for people to win - and win big.

Something that has helped me a great deal is waking up and showing gratitude for all the things I have gone through positively and negatively. Most people only celebrate positive breakthroughs. What I have found is that it's the negative events that put us all in positions to be successful. Think for a second about every wonderful event that happened to you. If I had to guess, each event was tied to a learning experience out of something negative.

We all have to learn how to monetize our mess.

My parents taught us so many principles through their actions and not as much through their words. When I really sit down and think about it, showing someone instead of telling someone is the best way to teach. When I taught second grade, my students were not that much experienced. It was my job to train them and fill in the life experiences that were missing.

That philosophy is very similar to the village mentality we need to adapt to our communities. If we all take care of the village in the beginning, we would get a much different result. Right now, it's every family for themselves and it's just not effective.

One thing that my parents mastered when I was growing up was introducing me to well-rounded individuals so that I could learn from everyone. I also learned from a few of their friends what not to do when I grew up. Both examples were important in my growth.

The moral of the story it is not how you start, it is how you finish that is more important. Also, if you had a bad start in life, you can still create a new beginning. You can change the frequency of your life if you keep your mental (Where you want to be in life or your vision for yourself) and physical (where you currently are) in two separate places. This means that if you are struggling financially, in your mind, you should be a mental millionaire.

Most people are in mental bondage, so your physical normally follows your mental. I have learned to keep those two separate as much as possible. When the two were in the same place, awful things tended to happen to me. Once I separated them, things started to change instantly.

If you need a new beginning, then start now and make a decision. Once you make a decision, then don't ever look back. Celebrate your new beginning. Also, start waking up with a prayer every morning that should include a gratitude affirmation. This will start a blueprint for success for the rest of your life.

Most people complain about everything that is wrong in their lives instead of celebrating what's right. The time is now to give birth to the new you. Look at today's date. That will be your new birthday. This is the day that you decide to create a new beginning. Congratulations on a new you!

Chapter 2: How They See Me

People always say that race does not matter. Everyone, no matter what race, should be treated equally. That's what the American Dream is all about. Over my lifetime, I've learned that theory is absolutely false.

I can vividly remember many instances where I was harassed because of my race. I grew up in a diverse neighborhood and I really don't remember too many specifics until I got older. By that point, race seemed like the only thing that mattered.

One Friday, I was traveling on Route 13 in Salisbury, Maryland, when I was stopped by the police three times within 45-minutes. At the time, I was a college student returning from work. Two of the three officers asked me if I had any drugs in the car.

I instantly knew why I was being pulled over: DWB. 'What is that?', you may ask. It stands for "Driving While Black". Throughout my life, I have been pulled over tens of times with no probable cause. This is frustrating but just proves that this is how the world sees me.

When I owned a real estate company, clients never even knew that I was the owner. We had clients of every race, but I knew that we would do more business without me being in the forefront.

I always had to play the race game in my life. It doesn't feel good to have others discriminate against you. I realize not all people are like that, but it makes it hard for those of us who are not. They say one bad apple can spoil a bunch. In my experience, that is very true.

One night I was driving in York, Pennsylvania, and a cop pulled me over because he thought I was drunk. It was odd because at the time, I hadn't had a drink in over ten years. So, the question is: why did he really pull me over? My guess is as good as yours.

I have plenty of mentors and friends from different races. After one of them heard the story of me being pulled over, he could not believe what goes on in my world.

I believe people are insensitive to how things like this affect people. The world needs to embrace diversity. Every business venture, neighborhood, mentor, and friend has had plenty of diversity to succeed.

In 2013, I decided to move into a 10,000 square foot home which had everything I desired. The first week I lived there, the majority of the vendors asked if I was there for the Baltimore Ravens' training camp. I wanted to ask them why they asked but never dared to do so.

People need to stop assuming that blacks are not competent enough to own a business and become successful without pushing drugs. Every racial encounter affects our race. Even looking at our justice system, there applies a different set of rules for certain races. I have seen harsh sentences given out because race played a part. Unfortunately, it's the way of the world and hopefully, we as citizens can implement change to shift the culture.

I always have a victorious mindset and never allow myself to create excuses. Once you start doing that, it's over.

When you know your truth, make it hard for people to deny you.

There have been so many killings of African Americans around the country by police. I have never seen anything like it. I pray that everyone in the world chooses the side of what's right. There is so much built-up hatred that is now starting to become the norm.

We witness mass shootings in public places, and the media does a phenomenal job of controlling the minds of the public. The things they show on TV are outrageous. Even kids' programs have hidden messages! Parents should monitor everything their children watch. These programs are designed to shape our future and the minds of the world. They are also used as a tool to push political agendas.

I have realized that the federal government's goal is to take as many people in the African American community as possible and assign them federal numbers. This will help the population. When you take fathers out of their homes, it leaves a race lost and dismantled.

I remember sitting in a young white male's court proceedings years ago and heard how the judge spoke to him. I was shocked! She was very patient, directed him what to say, and ended up not putting the crime on his record. I have also witnessed a rape case in

Texas where they sentenced a young white male to only six months. If that had been a black man, he would have received 8-15 years in jail. That is the injustice I speak about.

This book is not about race, but let's face it: there is no equality in the world. It seems like sometimes the only thing that does matter is race.

I thank God for the mentors I have had over the years. They saw me for me - and not the color of my skin. They demonstrated what the world should be like and how we need to treat each other. I just wished the rest of the world could take a page out of their book.

It's important to understand everyone's culture because you never know when you will need someone's help. I never believed in pigeonholing myself by only dealing with my race. I feel like I am a global leader and will bring change to the world.

How does a change start? It all starts with one's self first.

After changing one's self, we can bring about change. Once we make a decision to start diversifying our circle and be open to other cultures, it's amazing how much we can learn. Just being open to other cultures and receiving the information is enough.

My mindset has always been to represent my race. I want people to think differently about who we are and what we are. Normally, I don't like to speak about this topic, but it has become a major problem in the country. It is time for a change.

What we should not do is use racism or racial profiling as an excuse for why we are behind. Everyone and every race should get inspired to become a part of the change.

The one thing I love about sports is that it brings everyone together. Sports promote unity. I love football and have been attending games for over 20 years. I have met so many people who have something in common: a love for the Baltimore Ravens. Every Sunday, we celebrate, get mad, cry, laugh, and felt awesome together. No one thought about race or segregation. We traveled to the games together and had fun. That is how the world should be. I pray we can get back to it.

There are so many places where people use racial profiling. I remember walking into restaurants and waiters ignoring me. Others didn't want my table because they thought I wouldn't tip. Little did they know I always tip 25 percent and over.

I have always had the attitude that I would be ten times better in whatever I did. That's how my parents raised me.

I still think there is hope that the American people will come together in unity and make this world a better place. The residual effects of racism has left our communities in shambles and may deter African Americans from living their best lives.

Chapter 3: Frenemies

Sometimes friends can be overrated in life. When it's good, they are great to have. I have always attracted people to me for some reason. Everyone will tell you that Andre Vaugh loves to have fun. That's just who I am and who I will always be in life.

I have had some amazing childhood friends. For this book, I will use fake names for them.

One of my tightest friends was a boy named Jordan. We met when I was six years old. We were both competitive. I remember playing hours and hours of basketball together. Jordan and I hung out all the time and had so much fun. One of my favorite memories is going over his house and eating sandwich spread on my turkey sandwich. We had a true love for each other. To this day when I see Jordan, it reminds me of that love we still have for one another.

I later met some key people in my life when I was in high school. I remember attending Woodlawn High School and meeting Charles and Kevin. We were all tight and had so much fun together. Kevin was a star athlete on our basketball team. We were tight and made sure that we had each other's backs. On the other hand, Charles loved the street and was the protector of the crew. I can't begin to tell you the things we used to get into growing up.

In tenth grade, I met another close friend, James. He had moved to my neighborhood when I was 15. We ended up being very close and had a wonderful bond.

Last but not least Rico, a childhood friend who ended up being my fraternity brother at the good old University of Maryland Eastern Shore. Ultimately, this was the crew: Charles, Kevin, James, and Rico. Growing up with them, I intended to be there for them no matter what. When I love, I love hard. If I had it, they had it. That was the bro code I lived by with these guys.

After college, I started to get the entrepreneur bug. I knew I wanted to be ultra-successful in everything I touched. I also tried to inspire everyone around me to never settle on just a job.

Once we started our journeys to be successful, things changed. See - to be on top of your game, you have to make some sacrifices. You can't spend like everyone else, nor go out as much. I remember making a decision to stop drinking. I didn't have a drinking problem, but a friend of mine said if you want to gain wealth, give up something you love for six months.

I followed directions and gave up drinking instantly. I was willing to do whatever it took to chase the American dream.

I also wanted my friends to be right there with me making things happen. The great thing was they started to work on making money and on being their own boss. It was amazing, and I just knew we would rule the world together.

Several years went by. They were all on their ways while I was rolling myself. I was taught that you don't give a person a fish - you teach them how to fish and they will eat for a lifetime. That made a lot of sense to me. Gradually things started to change in our relationships. All of them except Charles stopped hanging out with me. Rico even got married and left me off the list.

Now, I understand when two friends fight and stop talking. This scenario was different. I really didn't have a clue why he broke ties with me. This was puzzling and I didn't spend a lot of time trying to figure it out. When we saw each other, it seemed genuine. It was almost as if someone told him to stop talking to me. I heard he had made a statement that I was living in one neighborhood and he was living in another. I really didn't know what it meant, but I kept it moving.

I learned you can't give certain things a lot of energy. Elevation will cause isolation - and boy, was I being isolated!

My friend Kevin and I were probably the tightest. We had similar skill sets and were two peas in a pod. He was a straight shooter and I respected that. We got along really well because we both could hold our own in the world. Something happened once I moved back to Maryland and I didn't even notice right away. Kevin started having conversations about me and my success with others. When I first heard this, I was hurt but didn't say anything. I would never have expected Kevin to try to discredit the body of work I had put together over a huge period of time.

My friends were engaging in conversations about what I owned and saying I wasn’t really doing anything. I always wanted the best for my friends, but at some point, something changed. Even James, the godfather of my twins, changed and we fell out. We did a lot of business together and had rolled for four great years. The funny thing is that all of my friends were the type that had your back no matter what. Of course, losing friends like that would affect you, for sure. Success sometimes is overrated, and things will start to change around you.

Charles, my protector, called me a few days before I headed to prison to give me the ground rules. I will never forget that authentic conversation and it was much appreciated. Even though my relationship wasn't the best with my friends, certain events in life require a cease-and-desist on all foolishness. I remember James losing his mother and I was right there to support him.

I realized that with all my friends, there was nothing specific to warrant us not speaking, but things happened. I don't know if I was in the spotlight too much. I can honestly say everything that happened between us has confused the heck out of me. It couldn't be jealousy, because these guys were confident men with a skill set that was out of this world. That's why to this day, I am still confused.

When the news came out that Andre Vaughn was headed to prison for fraud, Rico and Kevin had a field day. They led the pack in spreading the news to anyone who would listen. This was their chance to validate why we stopped hanging out with each other. I can say I wasn't shocked that they behaved like this. Some people in your life want to see you fall. They won't show their character until you start operating with grief.

I remember my friend Julie bragging about how tight her friends were and that they have always had her back. I simply said that's because you have not done anything of significance yet. She was instantly offended and disagreed vehemently with me. It wasn't until she started to own her own business and make sacrifices that she noticed a change in her tight circle.

Pro tip: Start becoming successful and then pay attention to the people that are the closest to you. Some will support you and some will not. Rico and Kevin found joy when my family was down. When I heard about it, I was at peace because I realized I was freer in prison than they were out of it. They still had to go on living their lives with that resentment. Normally when people behave like that, they have a big void in their lives. I can guarantee my family is running better than theirs while I am in here. I know there is a reason why I am here, and I made the decision to make this work.

I think my biggest mistake was not talking about my struggles in business with my friends. Maybe they would not think that I was so lucky in life. I never believed in speaking about the negative things that were going on in my life.

I pray for Rico and Kevin every week. I remember saying to my wife that Kevin had argued with his wife more than we did.

Have you ever experienced friends who changed? Did their change surprise you? When major events happen in your life, you notice which friends and family stick by you and who doesn't support you. I want to encourage you to keep going no matter what happens with your friends. I call Rico and Keven "Frenemies" now.

I really believe that in the toughest time in my life, a simple phone call would have been sufficient. Just to check on my wife and kids if nothing else. I guess that wasn't an option when you have hate in your heart. There was a lot of chatter when the news hit, but the people I expected to call and check on me didn't. Those I didn't expect to call, did.

Life is about a bunch of curve balls and you have to be in the right position to handle them. I believe my friends wanted me to be a slave to them. They wanted me to make the sacrifices, put out the money, then give it all to them. I also realized that when you decide to do business with friends or family, you need to set clear expectations on that partnership. That's where I made the biggest mistake with my frenemies.

I never put any requirements or quotas to the business relationship. In their minds, as long as they were spending time that was good enough. I was never about production.

I have learned my lesson and will protect my friendships from now on. With so many people fading away, I said to myself it must be me. Everyone else can't be crazy. I started evaluating my actions and still couldn't put my finger on it. After a while, I concluded that my friends believed I owed them something and I was not fulfilling their financial dreams and goals.

I have always tried to put my friends in positions to win financially. I guess my expectations were for them to take it and run. I made Kevin the president of my basketball team and we were successful on the court. Once confusion started to happen with the team, however, I came to find out Kevin was the common denominator. Once he was no longer around, we still had the success without the confusion. I should have realized then.

Rico and James were a part of my network marketing business. I tried to help them with people and the business, and still, that wasn't enough. Sometimes you create a welfare system when you give family and friends things without letting them work for it. This will cripple relationships and have everyone depend on you. I encourage everyone to be an authentic friend without expecting any handouts from those you love.

Decide to be an asset in your friends' lives instead of a liability. Once you see your friends striving to be great, become their biggest supporter, customer, fan, and friend. Once we eliminate jealousy from this world, things will be better for everyone.

Even though I have frenemies, I still love every one of them and wish them well in life. I encourage everyone to operate with a forgiving spirit because it takes too much time not to do so.

Chapter 4: Singled Out

There is one day in my life that I will never forget. I was scheduled to attend a meeting in D.C., and for some reason decided to just stay at home. I was in the middle of a conference call, heard a knock at the door, and opened it. Standing there were two ladies in business suits identifying themselves as FBI agents. I was shocked, especially because I was in the middle of a call with my leaders.

I politely invited them in. In my mind, I wanted to be helpful. That was the biggest mistake I could have made. I should have had a lawyer present, but you live and learn. My leaders were concerned because I told them what was going on. I am transparent with all the people I work with.

Once I invited the agents in and had them seated, I concluded my conference call. They asked my wife and I so many questions. I had no clue why, but we steadily answered every one because that's who we are. The two stayed for about two hours and then left.

As soon as they left, I called my attorney because I was uncomfortable with their questions. The attorney practically yelled at me over the phone to never let them in without an attorney present. All they tried to do is build up a case against me.

At the beginning, I hadn't even considered this. I was just glad they left, and we could move on.

A year and a half later, I received mail from another attorney advertising his services. It said: Mr. Vaughn, I am sorry that you have been indicted by the federal government. When I read that, a brick dropped in my stomach. I was so confused and had no idea what was going on. My wife was being indicted as well.

This changed everything for me. It was one thing to be indicted, but quite another for my wife to be as well. I wanted her out of the situation at any cost. I knew she didn't deserve this, and our case was initiated by a former business associate.

I still cannot believe to this day how I found out about the indictment. I would think the government would notify us more formally - but they didn't.

Once everything sunk in, it was time for our family to get focused. There was no turning back and I was motivated to fight for my family. You see, they were trying to strip my family's freedom. I was not going to have that. It was time to go lawyer shopping, so we could find a good defense.

I made many calls and listened to each lawyer tell me something different.

This was frustrating and nerve-wracking. I was used to having total control over my life. Now I had zero control. My business partner even called me months into the proceedings with a lawyer recommendation, but at that time, it was too late.

I also found out that it was in my wife's and my best interests to get separate lawyers. At first, we could not understand why this was the case. Once explained to us that prosecutors normally use a tactic to make married couples flip on one another, we didn't like it. We never discussed this in length, but I can't imagine what was going through Monique's head.

After finally deciding on lawyers, all went quiet for several months. I was waiting on discovery, but everything was happening so slowly. The things that I received were bank statements I already had. I just wanted to see why the government was interested in me in the first place. I really had no clue but managed to wait patiently.

The problem with waiting is that your mind starts to wander and you get anxious. Different lawyers told me I should have gotten all of my discovery right away. Because my charges were based on bankruptcy, I reached out to the lawyer who worked on my bankruptcy and tried to get my files. He told me that they had all burned up in a fire.

My current lawyer said it sounded like a CYA (cover your ass). I was furious! How could a lawyer get away with treating a client like that? Here I am, charged with perjury in a bankruptcy case and my bankruptcy attorney would not provide my file.

It sounded like the government was playing dirty. At this point, I didn't have my discovery and could not get my file from the attorney. This was extremely frustrating, but I knew I had to keep my cool. The judicial process has a lot of holes and justice is not always served.

My wife was only connected with the case as a casualty of war. They had no interest in Monique, but because of our marriage, this was a prosecutorial tactic to get a plea out of me. My wife handled the situation better than anyone I know. She could have easily gone off the deep end, but she kept her cool.

When we first got the news, we were both confused. Every day we took care of the kids, community, and volunteered like crazy. We just wanted to be ordinary people.

Living under the radar has its benefit, but because of the gift God gave me, it's hard to accomplish. Here we are in the biggest fight of our lives and things were moving slowly and quietly. So many thoughts were in our heads. All I knew was that the sentencing guidelines for the crimes we were accused of committing, carried a maximum of five years and a $250k fine.

Finally, in November I got a call from my attorney saying the prosecutor wanted to supersede the indictment on me. That carried a maximum of 20 years. Apparently, they had interviewed a mortgage banker who said that he never wrote me a pre-qualification letter for a mortgage and didn't even write loans for that matter.

I was shocked! I had the e-mail trail for the banker, who was referred to me by a friend in Florida. I couldn't even wrap my head around the fact that this banker lying to me. I didn't know what the FBI said to him to convince him to lie, but twenty years away from my family was not an option.

I knew the government would do anything and everything just to get a conviction. In the federal system, if you go to trial and are found guilty, they will sentence you even worse for making them spend more time. That's why the feds have a 95% conviction rate: most people take a plea because they don't want to take the risk and go to trial.

I have an entirely different outlook on people who are indicted. We tend to judge people without first knowing all of the facts involved. After sitting with my attorney and wife for hours, we decided to take a plea deal if they would recommend Monique get probation. I did not want to chance my wife serving any time because of my mistakes in business. It was the right thing to do and protect our twin girls as well.

Our girls were used to Daddy always being around, but I also traveled a lot. Mommy was the one who was always there, and I knew this could make or break the Vaughn family.

We began the process and I remember my plea agreement coming in first. I was so irritated that I was signing it because I believed that I was truly innocent. Simply put, the government accused me of leaving off a bank account in a bankruptcy proceeding on purpose for financial gain. I was unaware that the account was even opened. It had no money or transactions in it. In addition, I owned a business that was not functional but wasn't properly closed. This was an administrative error, but because I was being charged with a federal crime, it meant much more. On top of all of this, I never actually went through with the bankruptcy.

All of this got under my skin, but I had to make decisions based on the best interests of my family. I remember getting the court date to officially plead guilty and accept the plea. I showed up and the normal judge wasn't there - I had to plead in front of a different judge.

After all was said and done, I couldn't help but think that I had quit. I felt so uneasy. At the end of the day, I had to remind myself that what I did, was best for my family. Now I was just waiting on my sentencing date to find out how much time they would give me.

Meanwhile, I let my business partners and friends know what was happening to me. I began to get so much support from everyone. I would need that support as I thought more and more about the worst-case scenario and being away from my family for a long time. We had spent so much time together.

I initially got my sentencing date in March but received three letters in the mail that postponed it. Because of that, I was able to attend an important business convention and celebrate my birthday with the family. Who wants to celebrate their birthday in prison?

At last, the sentencing was here. I had a phenomenal support system, including family, friends, and business partners that had traveled far to see me. Normally, when you go through something like this people will judge you and turn their back. But not in my case.

As the bailiff said, "All rise," and the judge entered, my heart started to beat quickly. I knew I had to be strong. My biggest concern was the probation officer recommending 24 to 30 months. My attorney felt she had miscalculated the offense, so the judge had to rule on that first. There were a lot of moving parts in these proceedings. Both attorneys presented their arguments and thank God the judge ruled in our favor.

Now the time had come for sentencing. The federal prosecutor started to present his case. As he spoke, I thought he was talking about some other person. When he had finished, he brought the bankruptcy expert in to give input. The judge was listening and nodding her head. I didn't know if that was good or bad.

My attorney then addressed the court and called witnesses. What puzzled me was the bankruptcy expert. He was very unorganized, and the judge began to cross-examine him. She asked if it was normal for a person to file 2-3 bankruptcies, and he said yes. Then she asked the prosecutor what made him pursue this case. The prosecutor said he had received multiple anonymous emails stating that I had hidden assets - not true! It was one person who sent two emails with nothing but lies. Enough lies to investigate me.

The judge said on record that in 20 years she had never seen anyone prosecuted for something like this and she didn't want me to feel singled out. At that moment, I knew what the title of my book would be!

I knew I wasn't crazy and when she made that statement it confirmed this is what God had ordained. My witnesses painted the correct picture and I could tell that the judge unwillingly gave me a 10-month sentence. That was the lowest guideline sentence she could give. I knew this was something I needed. When she hit the gavel, I looked at my wife as she shed a tear and realized this was the best thing for me. The judge knew it wasn't right, but, because I had pled guilty, she had to act accordingly. The judge also wished she was more involved in the case earlier. This made me feel vindicated. The judge saying, I should not be singled out and wishing she were involved earlier in the process gave me hope.

Unfortunately, this happens every day in our judicial system where over-zealous prosecutors try to keep up with high conviction rates.

When you commit a crime and hurt others, you must pay restitution. In my case, my restitution was zero dollars because no one was hurt. The funny thing is that I never even went through with the bankruptcy.

Being singled out was not fun but I appreciate the experience. I know that I can do something to change this injustice in America. There are so many families affected by this every day. We need to work together as a community to fix this. It's easy to ignore and move on with our lives, but this could very easily have been you or one of your family members in this same situation.

I am grateful for the experiences that I have been through. One of my life missions is to make sure we decrease the number of people who are wrongfully convicted of crimes so that more families are not separated as mine had been.

Chapter 5: 48 Hours

It's crazy that this chapter is titled '48 Hours' because there was a movie that I loved with Eddie Murphy titled the same. The movie had Eddie Murphy getting out of prison for 48 hours to help Nick Nolte catch some criminals. My story is slightly different, but it unfortunately also involves prison.

I vividly remember the week of my surrender date. I had so many mixed emotions knowing that I WAS going to prison. I started to think about all the criminals out there that were free - and Andre Vaughn was now a felon. Just waiting to serve a 10-month sentence for a white-collar crime.

I could not imagine being away from my family for that long. Monique and the twins had to attend a gymnastics camp that week and left on Wednesday morning. I was adamant about making sure they had everything they needed for the trip. That night, the twins slept in my bed and I let them eat cake and ice cream. They were pumped up for sure. At midnight, I ran to the store to buy them snacks for the trip. I wanted to do everything possible to compensate for the time I would be away.

The morning finally came, and they were gone. You see, I had never been away from my family that long. We all gave big hugs and kisses and waved each other off, knowing I wouldn't see my twins until the next year. After they left, I had to tie up some loose ends and mentally prepared myself for this test in my life.

The next two days went quickly and finally, it was Friday. This was the day I needed to report to Allenwood Correctional facilities. For some reason, I dragged my feet to leave. In my mind, I wanted to report at 11 a.m. I found every excuse to prolong my trip. I started to do last minute errands and procrastinate reporting.

Then my mind started playing tricks on me. I am claustrophobic and was unsure of the processing procedures. My business partner and friend called me and asked if I was ready. I was thinking, 'heck no' but certainly did not want to be a fugitive. So, we proceeded to the prison.

My stomach was in knots and I had lost my appetite. We got closer and closer and because it was 12:30, I figured I'd better eat something, not knowing when they would feed me. We stopped at good old Wendy's to get a sandwich. I got more and more nervous since I had to report by 2 p.m. and I was pushing it to the limit. These were my last minutes before I was going to lose my freedom for 10 months.

During the ride, I received many encouraging texts and people wishing me well. Sometimes it's the small things that make the biggest difference. They sure helped my nerves during the ride.

At last, I arrived at the facility, located in the middle of the mountains. This particular prison has three levels: low, medium, and penitentiary. I made one last call to my wife to tell her how much I appreciate and love her. She has been a ride-or-die wife during the entire process. We hung up and I went into the building. As I got to the door, one of the correctional officers stopped me and said to wait because they were bringing in an inmate. I thought I was bringing myself in as well.

I waited for thirty more minutes, then went in. I entered into the lobby and used the bathroom, not knowing the next time I'd be able to use it. I walked up to the front desk and identified myself as a self-surrender. The CO told me to just have a seat in the lobby.

By this point, I had been waiting a long time. Maybe they didn't want me here. I would have been fine with that. I started to get concerned when the clock read 2:15. I didn't want to get in trouble. Finally, four COs came in to process me. At that moment, for the first time in the entire case, I felt like a criminal.

They first escorted me to medical, then told me I had just missed the people who had to test me. One CO also told me that I had arrived on the same day when Trump had laid off 1,000 officers. This saga was about to get very interesting.

The CO told me I'd have to stay in the Special Housing Unit (SHU) until Monday without a cellmate. I was so new to this that I didn't even know what he meant. At medical, they gave me a quick check-up and TB shot - I wasn't happy about that. We left to do fingerprints, take photos, and receive my ID card.

After that, I had to change into my "prison wear" and shit got real. Just as we left the building, I was instructed to put my hands behind my back. I was confused because I had never been handcuffed until now. I got cuffed up super-tight and the personnel escorted me to the SHU.

Once in the SHU, there wasn't an open-cell, so I stood in the holding cage which was just big enough to fit me standing up. I could not believe they would put a human being in something like that. They threw clothes in there so I could change again into the infamous orange jumpsuit. I didn't realize it at the time, but I was going into solitary confinement!

I was in that cage for 45 minutes, and my claustrophobia began to kick in.

God kept me calm, cool, and collected. I even started to sleep standing up.

At that point, the captain came in and began to ask me all sorts of questions. After I was done answering, I asked when I could use the bathroom. I'd do anything just to get out of there. The CO yelled, "Vaughn, we're getting a cell ready for you". Thank God.

After another 15 minutes had passed, they finally got me out of that "slave cage". I cuffed back up and they walked me thirty steps to a cell. I felt like I was treated like a murderer as they escorted me to my weekend home. I was backed in the cell, in cuffs, and they closed the door. They told me to put my hands through the door so they could take the handcuffs off. Can you imagine what was going through my mind? It was almost like God was trying to break me down to my lowest point until he built me back up.

I asked the CO when I could shower. He simply said that I wouldn't get to shower until Monday when I left for the compound. Was he serious? Monday was unacceptable in my mind. I had hoped it would be right away. That meant I wouldn't be leaving this cell for another 48 hours. Even when inmates are in the SHU for disciplinary reasons, they got a chance to take a shower and leave outside an hour a day.

I realized my family and friends would not be in contact with me while I was back there. I could feel everyone worrying and wondering if I was alright. We are all used to communicating every day, so this would be rough.

The very first thing I did was take off that orange jumpsuit. That had to go immediately. Then I started to train myself mentally. I've trained many others in the past to never keep your mental and physical in the same place. Now it was time to take my own advice.

I sat on my bed just thinking how I ever get to this place. I am a firm believer in taking responsibility for your actions. It's just hard to swallow that I am in prison for leaving open a bank account I didn't even realize I had.

I knew in my heart that this entire process was ordained by God. I knew that God wanted my full attention in this hour.

That weekend was the longest of my life. There was no one to talk to. Nothing to read but my orientation book, which I read from cover to cover. All I did remember was the sound of prison keys. That's how I knew when it was time to eat. If I never hear keys again, I’d be just fine.

I completely lost my concept of time. I had to guess the time based on the meals and when they were received.

This was the first time in my life that I had this kind of free time. I decided to get plenty of rest and read the orientation book a million times. I also memorized my registration number with the BOP.

Friday was rough because I knew my family would be worried. I really wanted the day to be over so I could get some sleep. I knew then that another day would be behind me. I also did a few exercises to pass the time.

It was so important to me, in that moment, to appreciate the fact that I wasn't in that cage anymore. Sometimes, you just have to look at the positives instead of focusing on the negatives.

Friday was finally over and Saturday was here. The interesting thing about Saturday for me was that it was the first full day I was in prison. I still had no communication or concept of time.

The prison guard opened the door slot and gave me my breakfast. I made sure to say thank you every time I saw them. One time I didn't start eating and the guard told me I had to eat right away. I simply said 'okay' and 'thank you'.

I was on a quest to get whatever I could out of this experience. I made up my mind to serve my time and not let the time serve me.

Saturday went so slowly and seemed to take forever. I made sure to work out every day for two hours and then read that stupid manual again. I also took naps every four hours. It was so boring, and I was ready to go to the general population. Luckily, I did have a bathroom in my cell. I noticed every time I went to the bathroom, a guy who looked like Harry Potter would look into my cell. That was super creepy for me.

I always had a lot of people around me on a weekly basis and maybe God was now going to get my attention. Months before I self-surrendered, my family and friends organized so many gatherings and dinners for me. Overseas military and basketball players have to go through the same thing.

Being in that cell really put me in a position to reflect on how I ended up there. Just a month ago, I was being celebrated as the top ambassador in my company. Now for the first time, I became a liability.

The one thing that got me through Saturday was reflecting on the recent memories I had with family and friends. Sometimes, you need to be still and revel in the moment. Well, I was forced to be still for the first time in my life.

Saturday night came and the CO collected the dinner trays. I asked if he had any books that I could read. The guy in the cell next door offered a book and I got excited. I looked at the cover and thought to myself, 'I would never read anything like this'. At that moment, it was all I had. I was going to take advantage of the entertainment. I started to read, and for me, it was the equivalent of watching a movie. I read that book like it was the last thing on earth. I never knew how reading could help the time fly by.

Before long, it was Sunday. This was the last day before I left for the general population, so I visualized leaving that cell. Sunday was very quiet, and I had enough rest by then. I really missed my family and I knew that my wife and friends would wonder if I was doing okay. I had not spoken to anyone since Friday afternoon.

I continued to read while other cells were having conversations back and forth. I tried to just tune everyone out and stay in my little world. The only good thing about what I went through is that I didn't have a cellmate. Because of this, I was able to really reflect and get in tune with myself. I knew God was still in control because I had not lost my mind.

It finally got dark Sunday evening and I knew I would be out of the cell on Monday morning. I remember thinking about what it might be like around other people who were all here for different reasons. It was important that I kept the company around me to a minimum. I had to make sure I was focused on God's plan for me.

Sunday night, an inmate threw something under my cell door. I remember kicking it right back out the door. I didn't know what it was and didn't care. I wasn't having that on my last day in the SHU.

I couldn't wait to go to bed so I could wake up and finally leave. Besides - I had not been outside, let alone out of that cell since Friday.

Monday came and I was excited to experience daylight. We really take for granted the small things we are accustomed to, like fresh air. Also, the freedom to do what you want when you want to do it.

The CO brought me my last meal, but I wasn't really hungry. After they collected my tray, I started to exercise. Immediately after, I washed up with anticipation of getting out.

Finally, I heard a CO say, "Vaughn, get your stuff ready". THE MOMENT WAS HERE! I jumped up and was ready to call my family and friends. I knew they were going nuts by now. The CO came to my cell, thought I wasn't ready and left to come back in a bit. I quickly grabbed my blankets, glasses, handbook, and sheets and balled them up in my hand. The CO came back and asked me to put my hands through the door to cuff up one more time. Not again. I thought I was done with handcuffs. I left the cell, went back into the tiny cage, and changed into clothes for the compound. This cage was a bit bigger than the first one they had me in. I was ready.

These 48 hours completely changed my life. Every fear I had happened to me, but God had my back. I knew this was where I needed to be at this time in my life. It was meant for God to disrupt what I was doing so he could speak to me. This was the first time I can remember that I had a chance to listen to the voice of the Lord and watch him work without any distractions. This will go down as the best 48 hours of my entire life.

Chapter 6: Much Needed Vacation

Usually, when people think of a vacation, they think about a sunny beach, relaxing & reading, and spending time with the family. My first day of vacation was when I got released from the SHU into general population in prison.

From the start, I knew that God had ordained this vacation and I was dead set on making sure I used this experience as a means for relaxation, personal growth, and rest. You see, for twenty years I have been ripping and running from business to business. I have helped people nonstop, and by this point, I was just tired. Even though I felt I didn’t deserve to be in prison, I knew God needed me to take this 10-month vacation. God is a gangster and will sit you down if need be. So far, this is the best vacation that I have ever taken.

On my first day, I remember going to the place where I would be living away from my family. I reported to the Union B unit, where they issued me a bed and cell. Walking down the hallway was intense. I was the new kid on the block. I knew that inmates were wondering what I was there for, where I was from, or if I was a snitch.

The very first person that I met was my cellmate. He was from Mississippi and asked me where I was from. I said proudly, Baltimore, Maryland. He then led me to another guy from Baltimore. The hospitality was first-class for sure.

In prison, I learned it is all about where you are from. People from Baltimore made sure that I had all the things I needed for my first day in prison paradise.

I would like to repeat that it is so important to never keep your mental (vision of where you want to be) and physical (where you currently are) in the same place. Physically, I was in prison but mentally I was in paradise.

When I looked outside, there was nothing but mountains everywhere. The view was pristine - except for the barbed wire fence surrounding the facility. I knew during my vacation stay that I would get the most out of it.

Normally, the first couple of days of vacation are to settle in and get plenty of rest. As you already know, my first 48 hours, I got plenty of rest. I was now ready to see the amenities this place had to offer.

People always ask me how I could be so positive during this horrible time of my life. Deep down inside I knew God ordered these steps for me. My life was headed in the wrong direction and this scared me. My faith grew the moment I found out about my indictment. You see, sometimes you have to be open to change. Even though I was doing well in business, I privately believed that I was headed to a place that I didn't need to be. Some of my past business relationships were pretty horrible. God really needed me to evaluate what I was doing business-wise and personally.

During this entire process, deep-down inside I was ready to get this over with. I didn't want to go against the will of the Lord. I really knew this God-sanctioned vacation would take me to an entirely different level, personally and professionally.

As weird as it sounds, I was excited as well. I had some anxiety but was ready for a major breakthrough to happen. Andre Vaughn would not go to jail without something magical coming out of it.

I want you to think of something that happened in your life that you didn't like but you knew it would be good for you. That's when you know it's "grow time". Most people want all the lessons to feel great. Warm and fuzzy. The greatest lessons come out of pain and we must embrace God's plan.

Deep down, I knew this vacation would serve me. So, when all of my critics were taking shots at me, it didn't bother me. I knew what would come out of this process. The entire time I told myself that I am not here to serve time. The time is here to serve me. I am grateful God will help me leave this federal facility as a world champion. He has positioned me to be a better father, husband, business partner, and friend.

There were signs in my life that told me this was God, not the devil, doing this for me. He often disguises things to help take you to another level in your life. Elevation will require isolation in some cases. For me, that's exactly what happened. Every day I am in this place, I am grateful to God.

So many other inmates stay in the victim mentality mindset instead of a can-do-it mindset. This changes their entire stay. I often told my cellmate that I am in college because I was using this as a life-long experience to never forget.

The beauty of this vacation is that so many will be blessed by hearing about my experience. I pray that people will learn how to take their own mess and turn it into a miracle. The problem with our society is that we take small problems and make them into big problems. I trained my mind to take obstacles and minimize them. This helps those suffering from depression and mental illness, as well. Many of my family members ask how I have stayed so strong during this time of my life. The only way I accomplished it, is by knowing this time is an asset and not a liability. I could have said that I was in prison but instead I considered myself on a vacation or attending college. This is my way to put a positive spin on the situation. I refuse to give any joy to anyone who has meant harm or ill will towards my family and I.

It isn't easy, but I have focused on walking in greatness. God will get all of the glory from my time here. I know he was disappointed in me because I was operating at only 65 percent of what I was capable of. Most people don't fully exercise their gift and I believe that God will intervene to give a little motivation. He sure got me motivated!

God knew that I needed some quiet time, and this was probably the only way to get my attention. I know that when my vacation ends, I will appreciate my freedom and not take for granted the great gift God has given me. I will use my story to uplift others.

I know that we are all global leaders. Life and death are in the power of the tongue. What have you been speaking about in your life? Have you been positive in negative situations? If not, it's time for all of us to rise to the occasion and make something major happen in our lives.

Think about everything that has happened in your life. Did you really learn from it? We have to learn to take a mess and turn it into a miracle. I have grown spiritually from my vacation and continue to thank God for it. I will travel the world, training people on how to use the airplane approach. When you are on an airplane, which is about to take off, everything looks so big. It's not until you elevate where things start to look small. If you have the same thing happening to you, it is because you have not elevated to your potential. This will happen over and over again until you make a decision.

Most people will continue blaming someone else instead of taking responsibility. This is your time and turn to shift every negative happening to you while you read this book. Right now, you might be in the middle of a vacation disguised as a storm and you have a shot to overcome the odds. Now when you see it again, change it up and say, "I am simply having a vacation moment!".

Anticipating my time in prison was not easy for me. All I had known my entire life was family and friends. I had been wondering who I would meet during my time and was nervous to meet a whole new crop of people I had never met before. I can't describe the feeling of not knowing who I would meet and what they had done to land in prison.

Once I arrived in prison, I began to notice that the men around me were phenomenal. I began to get curious about what their stories were. I was in an environment with men who came from different backgrounds and upbringings. Can you imagine living with gang members, drug dealers, bikers, mobsters, and mafia bosses? Not to mention child molesters, etc.

I learned early on during my time to never judge any inmates for their charges. I can tell you if they hadn't shared their charges with me, I probably would never had known 90 percent of their charges by the way they treated me. After speaking with a lot of inmates, it seemed like the system had failed them terribly. Upbringing has so much to do with how you treat other people. I noticed when you live in a household with an only parent, things change. A lot of men told me they simply did what they had to do to make money and provide for their families.

I began to think about how I grew up with both parents in the household and always found trouble. I couldn't imagine operating without my father in my life. After spending time with so many good men, I realized our society has given up on them and there are really no programs in prison that exist to help them become better men.

Our prison system is geared to punish inmates - not rehabilitate them. The prison system loves to offer programming for inmates, but only inmates teach them. I guess this saves them money. The one thing I really didn't like is that they only try to prepare you for a job and not a business or a career.

Most inmates want to make a lot of money. Maybe having some business classes would be helpful.

Another observation about the good men here is that it seems a lot of them were subject to peer pressure of some sort. While talking to some of the guys, they were so pleasant. I couldn't help but wonder how in the world they got here. Sitting up late at night, talking about our dreams when we got out and researching how to get it done was a blast. The lack of resources at our disposal added to the fun. We went back and forth to the library and made copies as needed. It was the norm for a few good men.

It's sad how the media and television paints a picture that every inmate is an animal and can't be helped. That is so far from the truth. I realized why they really don't let the media or any cameras in federal facilities. Taxpayers would be very upset at the amenities that are provided to federal inmates if word got out.

I know I have learned from so many good men while I was incarcerated and will continue to learn from them. My biggest lesson was not to judge anyone. There are always three sides to every story: your side, their side, and the truth. Normally, you only get the story that benefits the one telling it the most. The majority of times when good men go through the prison process, your family and friends turn their back on them. The longer your sentence is, the less likely people will be in your life unless you have solid people around you. I have witnessed some of the good men who have experienced this while I was on vacation and it broke my heart. I had major mood swings because of this. That's what really motivated me to start a nonprofit to support inmates and put them on the right track.

The facility where I was placed, horrible in regard to providing a support system to assist these good men to re-enter the society. You learn to deal with it and finish up your sentence. There was so much pain inside many of the inmates at the facility. It appeared to be deeply rooted from years of disappointments they had endured.

Serving a prison sentence is stressful in itself, but to not have the support of loved ones is difficult to handle. There were certain men that were in prison for some form of child molestation and a lot of their families cut off all ties with them. I couldn't imagine having my family not contact me or even visit me because I made a mistake. Having no financial or emotional support. It doesn't matter how much money you have or had on the street you still need someone to send it to you.

What really helped my vacation stay was the amount of support I received while I was there. People encouraged me every day and I used that to fuel my fire. When I arrived at prison, I told myself I would not meet anyone there or get close to anyone. I was determined to work on all of my projects. I vowed for once in my life to be selfish. As weeks went by, I started meeting the good men and got involved in so many activities.

The first interaction I had, was when I was coaching a flag football team. One of the guys in my unit asked me to coach. I asked myself what he saw in me that would make him ask me for help. Then when the basketball season started, two different inmates asked me to coach their teams. For some reason, I just couldn't say no.

We ended up winning both the football and basketball championships. I guess that is my passion: inspiring men that society has given up on and letting them know they still matter.

The secret to any success is establishing a healthy culture around you. Once you establish a healthy culture, you can easily create a winning culture. I have done that in business and athletics. It was amazing that while on vacation, the good men of my semi-pro basketball team were winning as well.

You will know when you build a winning and healthy culture because it will sustain itself when you are not there.

Another thing that I did in prison was regular attendance at church and Bible study. There were so many good men there who were looking to get closer to God. I enjoyed seeing the progress inmates had accomplished since they were there. It's easy to get caught up in just entertaining yourself while in prison, but when you focus on building yourself up, that's where the magic happens.

Every day of the week I worked out at the recreation yard. I met many good men there, as well. I learned that some people were considerate, and some were not. Working out is where many of the good men worked on their physical appearance. Just by watching people work out, I could tell the character of others. What I loved about working out is that other men told me tips to improve my own routine.

The library was another place good men went to learn. It was wonderful watching inmates share information and resources for everyone to win.

There are so many things I can say about the good men at my facility. The lesson I took away from the experience is to never judge people who are going through a journey in their lives. Be a blessing and see how you can impact the people you know that are in prison or headed there. I know they will greatly appreciate it.

Chapter 7: Family Foundation

Family has always been everything to me. That's just how I was raised to be, and it has helped me throughout my life. Family should be there in good times as well as in challenging times, without judgement. I reflect on my success in business and it primarily came from the type of support I have received from my family.

I have been through so much and 100 percent of the time I knew that I could lean on my family. I know this doesn't happen in every situation, but we can all start somewhere. Can you imagine the anxiety my wife and I had when we first got the letter saying we were being indicted by the FBI? Many things could have taken over: shame, doubt, embarrassment, and even depression. You have to have a special type of family bond to be able to feel open enough to share.

Over 20 years, I have been running some type of business and having success. My family has been proud of me throughout my business career, and now I was headed to prison. That's not the easiest thing to deal with: one of your family members going away to a prison. Especially when you have a family as close as mine is.

I remember having a sit-down with my mother explaining to her that I was headed to prison. I waited several months before I shared it with her because I always wanted to find a way to bring joy to her life and not create stress. But the time came when I had to have a heart-to-heart with her. I remember her being so positive and supportive during our entire conversation. I was afraid that she wouldn't be able to handle it, and I realized that my mother is much stronger than I could ever imagine. I learned to never underestimate the strength of a mother.

After it was confirmed where I got my strength from, my mother instantly, in a soft voice, began to minister and comfort me. I remember thinking that I should have shared this with her much sooner. I remember throughout some of the toughest times in my life that I have encountered, both of my parents took a comforting role instead of being a disciplinarian. This really helped me get through those tough times.

The family foundation is critical in today's society and slowly but surely it is fading away. I have learned to use my family foundation to help me navigate life, especially when I am struggling. I called my older brother first when I found out my legal troubles. It was important to get some sound advice from him and I am grateful for all of his help. I would have done the opposite of what he advised me, had I not asked him, and it would have ended up costing me more time and money in the long run.

I am a very independent person and normally I make decisions based on what I feel and not take advice from anyone. This is an area that I have to work on, once I am released. There are a few situations that I could have avoided if I had listened to the loved ones in my life.

I have noticed that in my quest to leave a legacy, I have gotten caught up in the work matrix. Sometimes we can work hard chasing the American dream, all to sacrifice family time. We were taught at a very young age: God, then family, then everything else. I have to say I have completely been out of alignment, and will have to make the proper adjustments immediately. My intentions were always to take care of my family by providing for them, but I need to shift some things around.

After calling my big brother, my next call was my twin sister. She has been my ride-or-die since day one. What I appreciate most about her is that she remained as strong as possible during my trials. She is very emotional, especially when it comes to family. I remember her being out of the country when I had to break the news of having to go away. That was one of the toughest times for both of us. We have never been separated for that long period of time. This was a first for both of us. I knew that I had to be strong to give her the motivation to follow suit. During the entire process, she made sure she was available, and was there in whatever capacity she could.

My biggest issue with this entire process was my twin girls. My wife and I pride ourselves in parenting and we have been there for them since birth. Whatever they needed was provided. This would be the biggest challenge by far for our family. Our girls were so sweet and innocent, and I just couldn't bring myself to share with them the news that their dad and mom could be going to prison. That would have rocked their world. All of my decisions were based on the protection of them. I knew, based on how we raised them that it would be a major problem for them to deal with. We couldn't have been away from each other for five years. That simply wasn't an option for my wife and me.

It's funny how people tell you what they would have done better when they have not even walked in your shoes. When you are parenting you realize things affect children for a longer time - sometimes for life. I wanted to make sure we made sound decisions based on the future of our children. That's the problem in today's society.

We put too much on our kids while they are handling the stresses of the world along with their parents. I have witnessed so many inmates' children without their fathers. I can't imagine what they go through on a daily basis.

Monique and I chose not to share with our girls what was going on. People have mixed opinions on us being up front versus not sharing. If I could do it all over again, I would do it the same way. I realize that my kids will know later on because I will be speaking about it, but I don't want them to worry about their daddy. One of my twins already has a fit when I go on business trips longer than three days. I can't imagine telling her that

I have to go to prison for ten months. When I call home, I either talk to them before or after the recording - never during it. The recording says, "You are speaking with an inmate at a federal prison". That's the worst and gives a constant reminder where you are. I know that if my girls had an inkling that I was in prison, it would have made my stay here rough. Right now they think I am out of the country on a business trip, and that's where I will leave it.

Last, but not least, I want to speak about my wife. I really appreciate all the sacrifices she has made during this entire ordeal. She was simply a casualty of war. What federal prosecutors love to do is tie innocent people to your case, knowing it will be a higher probability for you to take a plea deal. This was another decision that people questioned. The average people would think, why in the world would we plead guilty unless we were guilty of the crime? But it is never that easy. When I thought about our girls being potentially without both of their parents, it made my choice easy.

I am grateful for my wife's support, especially because all of this was initiated by a pastor seeking my demise. This was the second time that he reported me with a bunch of mistruths.

The timing of this case came at a bad time in our lives. I was in the middle of fighting a big civil case, and I chose to make that my top priority. Most spouses would have been super upset and not supportive. She could have actually cooperated with authorities to save herself. She hung in there, and would not allow anyone to break our bond.

I appreciate Monique for hanging in there with me. Without my family this prison experience would have discouraged me, and possibly crushed me. People can’t believe how strong I have been during this entire ordeal. My secret to success has always been family. I feel like I am unstoppable when I have their support. I feel like I can conquer the world, as long as I have my family by my side. Even as I sit here now, I am planning my return, and it will finally put my life back in order: God, then family, then everything else. I vow not to get caught up in the work matrix.

I am excited about my family's future. The twins did so well while I was away, and I made sure that this experience made our family stronger than ever. Please - if you have to work on your family's foundation, do it now. Tomorrow is never a promise.

Chapter 8: Clueless

Linda Compton Vaughn

"You cannot make progress without encountering challenges. What you can have, though, are the courage, determination, and persistence to push through those challenges.

Do not wish for life to be easy, because that is a wish for life to be empty. Seek instead the strength and fortitude to live a life filled with meaning and substance.

Awaken again each day to the wondrous reality of your problems, possibilities, limitations, courage, gratitude, disappointment, generosity, and by sorting all that out, live. Love is a rich bundle of powerful forces and varied directions, with so many great options for living it well.

Find solid confidence in knowing that whatever you encounter, you can encounter with grace, with integrity, with a commitment to add more goodness to life. Though you cannot choose the strength or direction of the wind, you can decide precisely where it propels you. Welcome that wind as it teases, as it shifts, as it howls, and revel in the awesome energy that is life. You have much good to do, and here is your day, your opportunity to do it".

Written by Ralph Marston

Life is a classroom designed specifically to propel each of us forward. There will be obstacles displaced as opportunities, speed bumps, distractions, manipulators as well as imposters on the path. If we become too busy in the negativities, we cannot discern the devious behaviors being exhibited. It appears that when you have a plethora of goals to be completed, that's when adversity introduces itself. At this juncture, I had to put a halt on dental implants procedure to ready myself for an abdominal surgery. Recently, I had enrolled in a class on "How to Write A Book". That's when the information regarding the internal investigation of my son ANDRE became apparent to me.

I was numb, perplexed, devastated, and prayerful. God's amazing Grace hadn't brought me this far to leave me. Being more focused to be the problem solver instead of the problem was the top priority. I know that God can do exceedingly abundantly more than we can ask or hope for. Going to the throne instead of the phone is habitual for me now. I have been very prayerful during this dilemma. Praising God and seeing His Grace and Mercy prevail in his life was my focus. What the devil meant for evil, God will turn it around for his good. No good thing will He withhold from those who walk upright before Him. As Denzel Washington stated, "Some people will never like you because your spirit irritates their demons".

Time is clicking swiftly. My surgery date was imminent, and the court date kept being changed for ANDRE. Andre couldn't make it to my surgery procedure, which is quite unusual for him, but ANDREA was there. Imagine her waiting for the surgeon to come give her the results of my surgery and lawyers calling to question her about her twin brother. As a friend told me that God won't put on you more than you can bear. Thank God for a successful abdominal surgery and for allowing ANDREA and her siblings to be actively involved with my post-op rehabilitation. In spite of Andre's impending court date, he brought me breakfast and lunch as needed, carried me to follow-up post-surgery visits, and conducted business efficiently. Less than two months after surgery, Andre's court date was scheduled, and I attended the hearing.

I'm so glad I was in a haze because I didn't know the magnitude of what this court date meant. Here was Andre and his lawyer in front of the judge, pleading his case. Is this the same young man who has spoken empowerment messages in front of hundreds of people? Is this the same young man who has received hundreds of awards for outstanding services? Yes, this is real. God had led me to testify. With a quivering voice and impaired speech, I told who my son was. If it didn't come out with clarity, that was my intent. It is troubling to witness the extent that people will go through to defame another human being. Sometimes pauses must be made in order to learn some of life's most valuable lessons. Just because people are with you doesn't mean they are there for you.

Snakes come in different sizes, shapes, and colors. They are poisonous and will bite you. During this trial process, I had a dream on two different occasions about snakes. The first one was about a big fat black snake that was in the top of the ceiling and I was terrified. The second dream was about a long yellow snake that I was attempting unsuccessfully to house in a jar to no avail, so he just roamed around. Though I was leery, I watched him because of the fear factor. In life, there are snakes lurking all around us, but we must be prayerful and praise God as we gain wisdom and knowledge in this world called life. My prayer is that this period of isolation has resulted in the purging of some associations.

On July 16, 2019, Andre came to visit me before he was to report for sentencing. Grief and sadness totally consumed my emotions even though the outer appearance was indicative of strength and valor. I felt a great void at the completion of the visit because I knew it would be a while before I would receive a telephone call or a text message. But, I felt confident that God would sustain and protect him, the prison personnel, and fellow inmates. The question is, have we learned the lessons that are needed to be learned. Some of your greater gifts will become evident during this period of isolation. Remember, God has to sometimes isolate us before He can bless us. Jesus said, "And greater works than these shall he do; because I go unto my Father." God is going to catapult you to another level. Always remember this and I quote, "Grapes must be crushed to make wine. Diamonds form under pressure. Olives are pressed to release oil. Seeds grow in darkness. Whenever you feel crushed, under pressure, pressed or in the dark, you're in a powerful place of transition".

A magnitude of life's lessons has presented themselves to you and with God's presence, you have prevailed. Though problematic at a glance, you had the courage and stamina to advance into uncharted territories. The tests have been intriguing and arduous, but you persevered and accepted the challenge. Sometimes you were isolated, crushed, pressured, squeezed, but you didn't flinch. This has been a vast discovery period, and in this period, impersonators have been exposed. Though painful, this pruning period is necessary for advancement. As Maya Angelou stated, "When people show you who they are, believe them". What has been concealed will be revealed in due season. A leopard can't change his colors. Just continue to bloom where you are planted. You have encountered an absorbent amount of adversity but keep your head held high because in the end God distributes the degrees for graduation. Make sure you have fulfilled all requirements for graduation so no course will have to be repeated. Know that I love you and I have never stopped believing or praying for us as a family and community.

According to Dr. Bryan Schuetz:

"Life is like a camera. Just focus on what's important and capture the good times, develop from the negative, and if things don't turn out, just take another shot".

Chapter 9: Phase 10

On any given visit, you would often see me making my guests play Phase 10 card games with me. Everyone who knows me is well aware that I love to compete and win in everything that I do. I remember when I was a kid I got excited every time I won a game. It didn't matter who I was playing with - I was going for it at all times.

Winning is a lifestyle and I wasn't looking for any sympathy just because I was in prison. I wanted my friends and family to give their all and try to beat me. Other inmates used to tell my visitors not to let me cheat them. They wanted to see me lose.

What I love about Phase 10 is that you have to go through different phases in the game. Often you are on different phases than your opponent. You have to stay focused because at any time things can change very quickly. It's easy to go from winning to losing in just a turn. After being the person to finish their phases first, you are the winner. There were many times I was behind and came back to win right after.

Life is exactly like the game of Phase 10. You may think your siblings, friends, and coworkers are further in life than you are. I would caution you not to think that way. I have learned that you have to run your own race in life. One of my favorite stories is the tortoise and the hare. The hare thought he would win the race because he was much faster than the tortoise. Even though he was faster, he still lost the race.

Over the years, I have seen people get to places and things much faster than I have. Normally when you see that, you start looking at yourself, thinking something must be wrong with you. We should all be excited that someone else in your life paved the way for you. They have given you the blueprint for success.

When I think about this chapter, the number 'ten' is very significant to me. First, and foremost, I was born on the tenth of June. I was also sentenced to ten months in federal prison. My twins turned ten years old while I was away and it was in 2020: a double-double of ten. Ten is also the most frequently used number in the bible. The number ten signifies the return to center as a new cycle of life begins. In the Bible, ten is associated with law and judgement, symbolized by the Ten Commandments which give men guidance to right and wrong. Ten also exudes an air of confidence, optimism, creative power, success, and an ability to adapt to new circumstances. The angel number ten has the energy of both one and zero, meaning you possess the traits needed to be successful in life:

poise, confidence, inventiveness, determination, self-assurance, uniqueness, strength, and leadership. The number one is a symbol of leadership, authority, and initiative. It also is associated with a positive way of thinking, inspiration, and motivation to start a new phase in your life. The spiritual meaning of zero has to do with potential. Zero visually resembles a circle, symbolic of evolution, infinity, and endlessness. In numerology, ten represents independence, infinite potential, wholeness, self-determination, and exploration.

By now, I hope you can see why I love the number ten. Playing Phase 10 in the visiting room inspired me to name this chapter. I have been through ten different phases through my entire process.

The first phase I call FORGIVENESS. It was critical to first forgive myself for putting my family in this position. Every action has a reaction and I believe the reason I was in this predicament is for things that I have done that had nothing to do with the case. I also had a bad habit of giving everyone the benefit of the doubt without doing my research. I had partnered with a pastor years ago who actually initiated my prosecution. That was the second time he had done that. Maybe if I had done my homework,

I could have avoided this entire prison term.

I also needed to keep better records for sure. And with that, I needed to forgive all the people who used this tough time in my family's life to benefit for themselves. I couldn't believe how cruel human beings can be when you go through something. I also had to forgive the United States government. They spent money investigating me for years and even brought charges against me for not including a bank account in a 341 meeting for bankruptcy.

In reality, I never even used the account or had money in it. I didn't even know it was open. I have scratched my head many times wondering how many people have been prosecuted for something they never intended to do. I have found out this sort of thing happens all the time. I also had to forgive my attorney for my bankruptcy. When the FBI was investigating me, they contacted my attorney and he never reached out to me. When the indictment came down, I needed to gather information from him, but he told my defense attorney my file got burned up in a fire. He never provided one single document for me to defend myself. The only thing I realized is when you hold grudges against people, you only give energy to them. That also takes energy away from you at the same time. That's why I always start with forgiveness.

The second phase I had to go through was RESTORATION. I had been grinding non-stop for 20 years, chasing the American dream, and never took a real break. I went from one thing to another without restoring myself in the process. When I reflect over those 20 years, I sowed so many seeds in people. I had a large group of friends, family members, and business partners who all depended on me for something. It didn't have to be money, but it was definitely motivation. I was the master at filling others' tanks up and restoring people's beliefs in themselves. I failed to restore myself. Early in this entire ordeal I began to work on restoring and rebuilding a new me: a better version of myself. God sent me on this vacation for reflection and restoration and I will take full advantage of it.

The third phase I experienced was the TRANSITION phase. When everything sank in, the bottom line of this reality was that I had to serve a ten-month prison sentence. I had to transition my thought patterns to prepare for my departure. This was a very difficult phase for me. I spend so much time with my family that I couldn't imagine life without them. This makes you appreciate the small things in life.

Many times, we take for granted our freedoms. Once they are stripped away from us, only then do we realize it is a totally different ballgame. Transitioning from doing as you please to becoming property of the Bureau of Prisons can be very challenging. I made sure to create a transition plan so my head could stay strong. In this phase, I had to learn the transition both mentally and physically to survive.

The fourth phase is ENVIRONMENT. I knew once I self-surrendered at prison, my environment would instantly change. You have to prepare for something like this. I knew I would be forced to hang around people I normally would not be around on the streets. I immediately established a routine that worked best for me. I knew if I made sure I was productive, it was less likely I would get into trouble on the compound. I also had a lot of books ordered so I could protect my mindset. I had to create my own environment within the environment I was in. Even though there was a lot of negativity around me, I totally missed the majority of it.

The fifth phase was being SELFISH with myself. I had given so much to help everyone else, that now it was my time to help myself. I was going to make sure I paid my bills in the world and not anyone else's. I declined other people's requests to work out because I wanted that time with myself and no other distractions. Finally, I decided to make myself the number one priority in my life and it was all because I decided to be selfish.

The sixth phase is FAMILY. Even though I had a great family relationship there were a few things I wanted to improve. The secret to my success has always been the family support that I have had in every venture I participated in. When you know you have 100 percent support form family, the sky is not the limit. I looked at certain instances in my life where I had chosen to miss out on family to chase my own dreams. I used those instances to identify things that I want to fix in my life so that I can be poised and ready to implement new strategies with the people I love.

The seventh phase I went through was BUSINESS. I am so fortunate that the businesses I have were still going while I was in prison. It was important that the fruits of my labor would keep going while I was down. I also wanted to analyze everything I did, and see if I needed to eliminate anything extra from my plate. I noticed in prison that other inmates talk mostly about getting a job. I wanted to make sure that I had multiple businesses in my portfolio. I worked hard to research new innovative ideas to create opportunities for the masses.

The eighth phase was FINANCIAL. It's great to make money but if you don't know how to keep it, that part doesn't matter. I started to audit some of the money I spent when I was free and couldn't believe what I found. I was wasting at least six figures every year and never realized it. I instantly became motivated to get my financial portfolio structured in order, and make some financial changes.

The ninth phase was my EXIT STRATEGY. I had to plan out in my head, and on paper, what I would do once I was released. So many people leave here without a plan. I wanted to make sure my exit strategy was on point and ready to be executed. I knew I wasn't going to spend as much money as I had in the past. I made a decision when I got out that I was going to make this prison sentence an asset instead of a liability in my life.

The tenth and final phase was my RELEASE. This would be the start of something new in my life. Once I got released and walked out those doors, I knew I had to come through. Every sacrifice my family, friends, business partners, and church family made, I was going to make them proud for it. That's why God showed me that I needed to release my book on the same date as my prison release: May 17, 2020. This just seemed appropriate. Even though it was risky, I made the decision and stuck with it. My release was symbolic of me releasing myself from any bondage or anger I had against the system, along with anyone who had done anything to wrong me. I was ready to be released from any wrong-doing I had done, as well. I simply wanted a clean slate so I could do what I was gifted at doing.

Those were the ten phases I went through during this amazing experience.

Chapter 10: The Prison Experience

Going to prison was surreal for me. Never in a million years would I imagine that I would end up there. While I was there, I went through what I call the "prison experience". What follows is just a little of what I went through during my time.

One of my biggest surprises was how segregated prison is: It is segregated by race, where you are from, your unit that you live in, and the crime you committed. I had no clue there would be that much segregation. I knew that it existed in the world, but it is on an entirely different level in prison.

There was even segregation based on religion!

I vividly remember waking up on my first morning in general population to go to the chow hall. There were certain tables you sat at, based on which group you were affiliated with. In my mind, I was just interested in eating and could care less where I sat. Oh - I forgot to mention: it was also 6 a.m.

Everyone has completely different schedules in prison. Some inmates went to work-out as early as 6 a.m. This was surprising at first, but I found out that everyone has a different goal and agenda. Different days you had to change your bed sheets, based on what unit you lived in. There were so many moving parts to the facility where I was located.

One thing I disliked was the ten-minute move. They would allow you to move every hour for only ten minutes. You really had to know where you were going. It was very difficult to try to do two things during that ten-minute move.

Everyone around found ways to adapt to the prison life and just make things work.

The Board of Prisons has something called 'count'. This is where every day, five times a day, you have to report to your cell and be counted. Twice a day, at 4 and 10 p.m., there are "stand-up counts", as well. This is something that happens nation-wide in the BoP. If there was fog outside, there was an extra fog count after breakfast.

One thing that saved me was the messaging system. When I first arrived, I didn't know how the communication would be held with my family and friends. I think in my mind, I thought I would only be able to talk with them over the phone. Thankfully, you also had thirty minutes at a time on the e-mail messaging system. Once done, you couldn't log back in for another thirty minutes. The messages had about an hour delay, coming and returning back to you. So, if you needed a response, it would take at least two and a half hours. Even though there was a delay, everyone looked forward to getting emails.

The phone system allowed you only 300 minutes a month to speak with loved ones. That averages out to about 10 minutes a day. It never seemed enough, but again I was grateful.

Inmates also played games and watched plenty of television. The TV room was a place where inmates could relax. The biggest thing I couldn't figure out was that many inmates believed they owned the TVs. You had about ten televisions in the room and each one was run by the leader of a particular area. So, it was a big no-no to change the channel of the TV that didn't belong to your area.

The same rules applied to the chairs in the television room. Each area had designated seats you had to sit in. At least the inmates didn't play around with the seats or the televisions. I never got caught up in any of those games. The television I own is in my bedroom at home - not in jail. I couldn't believe the amount of value people would put on just a chair. I guess this was just part of the prison experience.

The rec yard was interesting as well because many inmates work out on a daily basis. They had everything you could want there, which was nice. Some amenities include a field, basketball courts, horseshoe pit, bounce ball, racquetball court, handball court, free weights, elliptical machines, football field, track, pavilion, and much more. This was the place where people released the most stress, for sure. They also had pool, ping pong, chess, cards, and plenty of exercising going on. Inmates could go anytime of the day starting as early as 6 a.m.

That was a part of my daily routine when I was on vacation. Every morning on the weekdays at 7:30 a.m., I went to work out. I loved working out because it gave me a chance to have some me-time. Although many inmates workout together, I preferred to do it alone. I had received many requests to join workout groups, but I was adamant about spending time with myself.

The rec yard had a lot of politics, for sure: especially with the free weights. There weren't just inmates working out on bars whenever they wanted to. You had to join a group and pray to find a bar to join. Overall, the rec yard was much more than I expected, and I was grateful.

Another highlight of my day was receiving mail. Everyone crowded around the CO's office while the CO put mail in the boxes. It's amazing how the small things really start to matter in prison. I remember getting mail 85% of the time. To inmates, it is a sign of love and reminds us that people are still thinking of us out there.

Prison seemed to slow everything down and you are able to critically analyze every action and make significant changes in your life. Outside looking in, I would never have thought that any good could come out of prison. I made sure to stick to my routine, especially working out and going to the library. This made days, weeks, and months go by fast.

Another thing that helped my vacation was visits from family and friends. I don't know what I would have done without them. For the first three months, they denied my wife visiting privileges, which was very difficult. I made sure that I didn't allow it to break me. I continued to use the time to build myself up. During visits, I was able to see many inmates interacting with their own families. I saw little children visiting their daddies.

I got very emotional during these visits knowing that I couldn't see my twins. I also took for granted that all inmates don't even get a visit every week - or even every month. The BoP sends inmates anywhere in the country, which makes it hard at times for some to see their families. It also costs a lot, as well.

The average sentence in my prison was about seven years. If you had to travel across the country, you could see how costly this could be.

Visits, for me, kept me connected just enough to the outside world without overwhelming me. The reality is when my visitors would leave and go back to their lives, I had to return to confinement. I was very appreciative that people would take time out of their busy schedules to see me. This was a major part of my rehabilitation.

Some inmates only got visits once a year. I know this affected them, especially if they were family oriented. I wish the system would really try to keep people close to their families. I can't imagine how kids are affected by this. My favorite thing to do was play a card game called Phase 10 in the visiting room. I love competition and it took my mind away from everything.

The prison experience was enlightening for me, especially seeing how a lot of the staff treated the inmates. You could tell the CO's loved the power they had, and most of the times they were not rational or fair. I don't believe many of the employees were happy in their home lives, so they brought it with them to the workplace. Certain COs were mean for no reason, and it was a no-win situation.

I used to see inmates get angry and upset about how they were treated and go off the deep end. It was all a psychological game and would require mental toughness to get through it.

The biggest frustration was watching the staff not doing their job when it came to your paperwork. I saw many people's release dates get pushed back just because their paperwork was not done correctly. I had to run back and forth for two months trying to clear up an issue. That issue should have taken no longer than a day. Through all of this, I learned to stay calm, cool, and collected, and remain patient with the process.

I can say that certain inmates had special treatment and were taken care of with the best jobs in the prison. I had one friend that was being released, and the staff gave him extra bonus money so he could survive financially. That kind of treatment was unheard of unless you were in that special group of people.

There is no such thing as equal opportunity in prison. You just have to mentally prepare and stay to the course.

One of the hardest things I had to deal with is people trying to get one over on you. Inmates will definitely test you to see how far they can go. People didn't know how to take me in prison. I just didn't fit the profile of a meek person, therefore people were reserved with me. Once people saw how I moved, everyone knew I wasn't struggling or in need of anything. My word was good, so people loved dealing with me.

I noticed so many inmates that always tried to get over on one another, and I always just shook my head in disbelief. I kept forgetting we were in prison - none of us just broke in here. There was a reason we were all in a federal prison. I knew many of the inmates would be right back if they didn't change.

Some inmates took programming seriously, and make sure they were attending classes. Others just played games, did their work out, or watched television all day. I used to wonder why inmates would watch live PD or jail reality shows, as if being in prison wasn't enough of a display. I started to see clearly how people return to prison.

One common question I asked people was. "What's next for you?" Most of them did not know the answer to that question - probably the majority of inmates. There was a small group of inmates that were very focused on their new life and were ready to tackle it. It was exciting to see this because it gave me hope that prison could change a person. You needed to have some ambition because if you depended only on the prison system to head that change, you would be very disappointed.

The reality is whether you are in prison or out in the world, you have to make some choices and then hold yourself accountable to get the job done. Most inmates were amazing people who just got caught up in the wrong choices. After interacting with many inmates, I couldn't believe they were even in prison for some of the crimes they were here for. I knew lack of direction and guidance was a big reason they were here. I pray inmates will take the time away from their families seriously and make a change.

During my tenure in prison, I made sure I kept to my routine and stuck to it. I wanted to remain disciplined and focused. I noticed time started to fly for me. I remember some of my friends used to be bored - but not me. I didn't care what other people did. I stuck to myself and didn't derail or allow anyone to get in the way of my goals.

Every morning during the week, I started my day with prayer. Once that was done, I checked my messages and sent out messages to friends and family. Then it was time for my 7:30 workout. Rain, sleet, or snow - I was there. This was my alone time to get my mind together.

After lunch, I went into the office. The library is the spot I made into an office: where I worked on this book and other projects I had in progress. After two months of keeping my routine, people started meeting me at the library. This distracted me, so I quickly put an end to that and got back on track. I am big on remaining focused through the distractions in prison.

After my time in the library and once the dinner was over, I often went to watch a softball or a basketball game. This would kill a little time and before you knew it, it was night.

I kept to this routine religiously and it really helped my transition in prison.

Every Thursday morning, I had a barbershop appointment, and on Saturday mornings I attended church when not on a visit. The weekend was definitely dedicated to my friends and family that visited me. I wanted to make sure my prison experience was serving me instead of me serving time.

This was not a punishment for me, but instead something that would save me, my family, my business partners, and my friends. I was so motivated to continue to make a difference in people's lives - no matter if they were in prison or on the street. The biggest thing I wanted to do is stay out of the way so I would not extend my vacation like so many people did here.

The prison experience was something I made sure had a positive impact in my life instead of a negative one. I didn't allow anyone to influence any of my decisions and I learned how to stick up for myself and keep my eyes on the prize. I am so excited for my prison experience as I will leave a legacy because of all I have endured during this process.

Chapter 11: When Business Partners Become Family

One of the biggest things that helped my transition was having all of my business partners behind me at my sentencing. Normally when people go to prison, they lose 90 percent of their business, along with the partners they are associated with. Under normal circumstances, that is understandable.

Once I found out the government was interested in indicting me and my family, I knew that I would have to sit down with all of my core partners in each and every one of my ventures. I have full transparency in my businesses and decided to continue this policy with this blessing.

Why do I call being in prison a 'blessing'? It is because I have a certain type of personality that thrives while moving from one thing to the next. I have gone hard non-stop for 20 years, and God knew I needed a break to focus.

I remember the first day the FBI knocked on my door. I was on a leadership call with my team and I let them know what was going on. I was shocked they were visiting me in the first place. My partners were family members then, and remain family to this day.

I have always believed in building a family-oriented culture. Most leaders look at their organization as a dollar sign and nothing more. That has never been my philosophy. When I choose ventures, I make sure to create an even playing field. I want every partner I have to be able to make money and take care of their families. That philosophy has helped me a great deal, while away on my God-oriented vacation.

I am so grateful for the amount of support I have received. It overwhelms me at times because I know many inmates here do not receive the same type of support. My mailbox is lit up every day with things my partners send me for encouragement.

There were a few ventures that I was working on while waiting on my sentencing. The biggest venture was a network marketing company that sold health and wellness products. We launched that company in 2016, and I was one of its top money earners.

When I first got my sentencing date, I was bummed out because I would have to miss my company's convention. It seems strange: I was headed to prison, and the biggest thing I thought about was being there for my business partners at our national convention.

God looked out for me, because he postponed the sentencing twice. In the end, I was able to attend the convention, acknowledge all the hard work that my partners accomplished, and celebrate with my family. I even ended up earning the title, 'Ambassador of the Year'.

I was excited, but at the same time I knew there was a chance that I would be away for months or even years. Everything was up in the air. My business family made sure they showed me love at that event. It made me know that I was in business with the right people.

Everything starts with the co-founder and the president of the company. I went to Utah and had to explain my situation to both of them. It was an emotional time for me because I never wanted to be a liability to them - on an asset. Once I shared my issues with them, I remember the co-founder looking me in the eyes. He said, "We've got your back".

My situation had nothing to do with him. It had nothing to do with the company at all. For him to say that, sent a chill up my spine.

The president of the company also happened to be my best friend of 14 years. His support was two-fold. We used to speak every day in the mornings. Both of their support made it so much easier to deal with everything going on in my life.

What company owner do you know that will have your back during the toughest time in your life? Will they continue to pay you for your efforts? This is the story I tell those I know. Don't pay attention to me. I am the distraction. Look at the two people at the top and watch how they had my back during the process. It was unreal, and I will be forever grateful for their continuing help.

I must also speak about the SOGTP group that I worked very closely with. These are the folks who run our organization and made it happen for me. When I was down and out, I expected people to turn their backs and move on to new opportunities. Not this group of my family members. God put them in my life for a reason.

When I first envisioned this chapter, I thought about them. One of the greatest things they did for me is to just stay in front and behind me for protection. The amount of letters, pictures, quotes, books, magazines, and love was overwhelming. They gave reports on what they were doing and even hosted the company's major event in my hometown of Baltimore, MD.

It left a major impact on me that my business was still going without me needing to be there. I have motivated and inspired people for over 20 years in that business. Now the motivator was being motivated. This took our bond to a new level and I was super excited.

At our national event, this special group of leaders showered me with gifts. They also wrote encouraging words to keep up my spirits. That is what makes my vacation enjoyable. That allows me to know that my family is taken care of at work while I am here.

It feels like it was just yesterday when I had a small group of leaders over my mother's house to explain everything in detail. What they may not have realized is that I only invite family members to my mother's house. They should feel very special.

Once I am released, I will work hard to get each and every one of these leaders in a position to retire in five years or less. A person never forgets when people are there for them. I want to say to my SOGOTP family: I love and appreciate all that you have done in my time of need.

The week of my departure they gave me a going-away party. One of my partners drove over 27 hours to attend. That made me tear up for sure.

A few days before my self-surrender, I invited some folks to Ruth's Chris Steakhouse so we could break bread one last time before I left for my vacation. We had such a great time, and I gave my last in-person address to them. I encouraged them to keep this party going in my absence.

They have changed my life, my outlook on business, and all of my partnerships. I cannot put into words how much I will forever remember and appreciate their impact on my life.

I also appreciate the corporate staff of my company treating me like their own family. They send me messages here at Allenwood, even before I arrived. My MLM ambassadors were supportive, as well. To all of these people, I would like to publicly say thank you.

I started a semi-pro basketball team league 3 months prior to my sentencing. We were on a roll, but it was very tough for me. I had just started this business, and I was about to go to prison. There was so much excitement, and momentum in the league and I wasn't sure how it would all turn out. I remember meeting with both of my business partners to explain my situation and how it could affect our business. They did not for one second have second thoughts. They were both 100 percent behind me.

This became the common theme in my life. Instantly, we decided to accelerate our business schedule. My new partners were both willing to carry the torch while I was away.

Our draft was scheduled for August: one month after I was supposed to go to prison. One of my partners instantly wanted to move up the date of the draft so that I could be there.

Here I am, going through one of the toughest times in my life and I felt great. My partners not only wanted to continue to do business, they wanted me to be there.

This new venture with a basketball league was completely different for all of the partners involved. The teams helped to purchase a franchise - and each of them stayed in the league. It was a much easier decision to have left. They could have requested a refund, and went somewhere else after learning about my hardships. They didn't, and I am forever grateful.

I first started the basketball league because the previous league lacked integrity. That became my motivation.

Once I was sentenced, a few team owners from the old league contacted the new owners about my prison sentence. It's amazing how people act when they think you have fallen.

Similarly, old business partners from my network marketing business went on social media sharing my situation and trying to financially benefit. This goes against my beliefs that no weapon formed against me shall prosper.

There is never a reason to elevate yourself by tearing someone else down. Everything that I do, I build a strong positive culture, and make sure I treat people like the celebrities they are. Having such close families in my business has helped immensely.

When I told my basketball players what I was going through, I asked them to use my situation as a learning experience. Never use anything you face in your life as an excuse why you cannot get something done. You could hear a pin drop in the locker room anytime. I provided them an opportunity to stay out of prison while I was on my way there. The support I received was simply incredible.

When you turn business partners into family, it makes life easier. Whatever you decide to do, create a healthy culture around you of love and positivity. Ask yourself: If I were headed to prison, would I have a support system that will work for me?

All of my partners were determined to make my vacation enjoyable. When I am released, I will make sure we all grow together. I have huge plans and I am committed to see them through.

'When Business Partners Become Family' is one of my favorite chapters in this book. I don't take for granted the love I have received from them.

I hope this inspires you to look closely at the partnerships in your life. If you need to make adjustments to your business relationships, now is the time. Set your business to run on a system with a strong, positive culture that you create - not on you.

When your business can run by itself without you at the helm, you know you have something truly special.

Chapter 12: Eye of the Tiger

Every time that I speak publicly, I enter to the song 'Eye of the Tiger'. Why has this been such a key part of my identity for the better part of 15 years?

When there are trials and tribulations in your life, you need to have an 'Eye of the Tiger'. When I hear that song, it puts me in a positive trance. Everything that was wrong instantly becomes right.

The opening line of the song says "Rising up back on the street, did my time, took my chances. Went the distance now I'm back on my feet –

just a man and his will to survive." Wow! Did my time and back on my feet. That meant something very special for me, and now means even more since I was sent to prison.

Every experience you go through, champion it. You have to make a decision between being a victim and being victorious.

When I faced difficult times in my own life, I made a decision not to keep my mental and physical frame in the same place. I trained myself to turn a mess into a miracle. I use any test and turn it into a testimony. I am blessed and highly favored. I never want to give any of my critics' satisfaction through my God-ordained storms.

This relates to the song. You have to go the distance in life and never give up whatever you face, and as the song says, you will be "back on your feet". I know this is easier said than done, but I am living proof that it is possible. It is more than just possible: it is a must.

The song goes on to discuss a will to survive. The last decade of my life has been filled with a strong will to survive. I often say that it isn't skill, its will. Most of my businesses I started without any formal training. I just made a decision and made it happen.

I want you to think of your greatest accomplishments. Was it your skill or your will that helped you the most? My guess is that it was skill. Many people have weak wills and try to compensate that with skills. This simply does not work.

Why do we place such a strong emphasis for our children to get good grades and attend college? We do this, but never teach them to not give up. When I think about the people who went to high school with me, the ones who got Cs and Ds are those who own their own businesses today. They may not have done well in a formal education, but they did well in the school of hard knocks.

I've been through so much, working towards success. Most people could never pinpoint when I was struggling. That is because I knew that attitude is everything. When you act positively, you get to your destination faster and more successfully.

This is what having the eye of a tiger means to me. Learning to dance through a storm. Realizing we need every season in our lives. Embracing the good and the bad.

Another part of the song says, "So many times, it happens too fast". Life will pass you by, if you don't stay ready. There are so many moving parts to life, so there is no sense paying attention to people who don't mean you well.

When I began my prison term, there were a few people I met who wanted to use my situation for their financial gain. Some business partners were irritated by how low people would stoop just to get ahead. I simply stayed calm and exercised the eye of the tiger. I was in a champion mindset.

Entering to that song on stage really taught me how to persevere through the toughest times in my life. I used it to channel my inner greatness and overcome all obstacles. Everyone can use whatever works for them during the toughest times in life.

When we don't deal with our issues head-on in a positive way, depression will creep up on us, without us even realizing it. Over 60 percent of people who suffer from depression don't even know it. Mental illness is a huge problem in our world. I encouraged everyone to be aware of themselves and to keep issues from creeping up by addressing them immediately.

The eye of the tiger has gotten me in trouble, as well. When I learned this skill, some friends and family thought that I just never went through anything hard in my life. That can quickly lead to animosity.

With some of my frenemies, I didn't even realize this was happening. It was a catch 22 situation. People don't like when you complain about your life, but they also don't like you when you don't need them. That's why you simply have to work on yourself. When you invest in yourself you start seeing personal, financial, and family growth in your life. You will start learning what the eye of the tiger really means.

Every industry I joined, I learned how to win. It wasn't because I had all of the skills. It's because I learned how to exercise the eye of the tiger. I trained my mind how to create a positive picture during the worst times in my life. Doing this allowed me to keep planting positive seeds, which then created positive momentum for me. This didn't happen overnight, but in time, it works if you work at it.

Once I knew I was headed to prison, I started exercising the eye of the tiger. I wouldn't stop even when people would give me permission to lose my mind. This was not just Andre Vaughn picking a song to use to enter the stage. This became my normal life, and how I dealt with situations that came my way. I have had so many people ask me how in the world I could stay so positive during this process. Once you truly learn the eye of the tiger you won't ask me anymore. I am determined to take this prison term, and bless so many people in the process.

This prison process has been ordained by God and not the devil. We are so quick to blame the devil for everything, when really God is just looking to get our attention. I will tell you one thing for sure - he has my attention. I know the gift he has given me will benefit me in the long run. I will use this for His glory instead of my own. I have been commissioned to use the eye of the tiger in this time-out. I finally get it!

Another line in the song says, "You trade your passion for glory". So many times, we work on success instead of working on our passion. That tends to lead to failure.

I have learned to simply stop doing the things that I don't like doing. I have passed on several opportunities because I was not passionate about them. It's no secret that I love having fun. Can you imagine truly being on fire about your job? Getting paid to have fun? Don't simply settle for a paycheck. Don't turn your passion in for glory. Don't ignore what you can accomplish by focusing on money.

I pray that more people will follow their passions instead of just chasing glory. When you hear "Eye of the Tiger", I hope you truly listen to the lyrics and get something special out of it.

The world has many moving parts. Many distractions. We are all here to make a difference and live our best life. It's time for us to focus on our own dreams and goals. We have the ability to create whatever life that we want. Society has done a fantastic job of keeping us away from our destinies. People get so distracted by social media, television, work, friends, and other entertainment. There is so much negativity out there on all of these platforms. Think about the negativity and what your life is like when you are consumed with it.

This is when you can implement the eye of a tiger and focus on things that bring positivity. Reading plenty of books and personal development are two keys to success. There have been plenty of times where I was stuck in a situation, but because I fed myself with positive things it all worked out for me.

Winning is a lifestyle. I expected to win in every situation. I am in prison and most people expect me to lose. The exact opposite thing has happened to me instead: I used this time to win. I am helping me, my family, businesses, partners, and my future.

My life could not be clearer: I am on an 'Eye of the Tiger' mission. Most inmates talk about what they will do when they get out. I speak about what I am doing right now, and will continue to do.

It is important to also hang out with people who have a similar positive mentality as you. When you associate with those with limited thinking, it rubs off. Friends and family members will begin to call you with their problems and transfer all their negative energy to you. I began to isolate myself from the negativity in my life, and increase my personal development, and that was the time when things got better for me.

I have gone through so much in the past five years, but learned to make it still look good. Most people, when they meet me, would not have any clue what I have gone through. Here’s the secret: when you are positive, and share the love you have for your business with two or three friends, those two or three friends will share it with two or three others. Before you know it, a few hundred people will be sharing the positivity and energy you have about your business. This will change your entire situation!

Once I implemented this in my life, things have been incredibly awesome for me. This is all in spite of my prison situation. The world has access to what I am going through because I am a public figure on social media.

Things that I would love to keep private, end up being public. Once you decide to just go for it, there will be more scrutiny on you.

Right now, I want you to start decreasing in order to increase. This means that you should spend less time on anything in your world that brings you negative energy. Decrease negative conversations. Decrease negative things you watch on television. Your subconscious doesn't know fiction from nonfiction, so you can attract negativity in your lives just from the things we watch.

Even if I love a show and it's a bit negative, I always try to follow it up immediately with something positive.

Watching the news is never an option for me. Watching the negativity on the news all day, then going to do a job just encourages the spreading of that same negativity. Then if your coworkers are negative, what do you think your bank account will end up looking like? Negative.

Use the 'Eye of the Tiger' to protect your space and your energy. Keep a level of focus, so you are able to conquer anything that comes your way. Soon, things will happen to you that may not have happened in a long time.

This will be your season of shift but will require you to focus for 21 days first. Once you accomplish that, increase to 90 days. You're now on your way to having the Eye of the Tiger!

Chapter 13: The Secret

In my lifetime, I have figured out a formula that simply works in every area of my life. This formula has helped me make a ton of money, travel around the country, and earn top-level positions in every company I have worked in. It basically has showed me how to flat-out win. It is a combination of things that we must apply every single day. It's almost like baking a cake. If you leave out the smallest ingredient, the cake won't taste right. This secret formula is something I have worked at for over 20 years of my life and am ready to share with you.

People believe that in order to be successful you have to be formally trained. That's just not true. As long as you have a secret formula and stick to it, you will be good. I think back on all of the sports teams that I played with as a child. We always had a winning record - even in high school, as well. One year, we had a perfect record through the entire regular season. In high school, I ran for class president and won. I taught second grade, and had the best classroom in the entire school. I got into the horse racing industry, and won five races in a row with four different horses.

My point is this: Once you master these attributes that we are about to discuss; you will be able to conquer anything in life and in business.

The first thing you must have is faith. It is important to be able to see things before they even happen. In every business venture I was ever a part of, I struggled in some areas. What helped me was I had enough faith that things would work out. I wasn't sure at the time how it would happen, but it always did.

The majority of people get discouraged and quit at the slightest sign of obstacles in business. Once you start having faith, you will be able to shift your outcomes.

I have always believed in a higher power in my life. God has come through for me in tough situations. I often reflect on how great God has been, and therefore it allows me to build even more faith.

After having faith, comes the right mindset. Both faith and mindset go hand-in-hand because they require having a strong mentality. I believe that my mindset is my strongest attribute. I have learned to remember every positive thing I have done, and keep it with me at all times. Even when I am having a bad day, I trained my mind to translate that bad day into a good day. When bad things happen to me, my mind sees it as something positive and not negative.

My business partners are confused as to how I can go to prison and be just as positive as I was before this happened to me. It is because I have worked at this for two decades of ups and downs in my life.

Let's imagine that you have faith and a positive mindset. Those are only two ingredients for taking your life to the next level. The next thing you will need is loyalty. I have seen so many people who are only loyal to themselves. If something serves them, they will be loyal to the cause as long as they personally benefit from it. I want you to think of a person in your life that is like that, and immediately decrease the amount of time you spend with them. That relationship will probably go nowhere.

Once you show people you are loyal to them, they will be there to help you do whatever you need. Having the right team behind you can mean the difference between failure and success in life and in business.

Once you learn faith, mindset, and loyalty, the next attribute to master is commitment. Success takes time. Most people don't stay committed long enough before it flourishes. If I am a part of something, it doesn't matter how big or small it is: I commit. I want the people who surround me to know that I commit and that they can count on me.

I often ask people how they plan to be successful if there is no commitment. When you are committed, you still give 110%, even when the motivation and inspiration isn't there. We have to sow seeds for success in any endeavor we participate in. This means to spend time with that organization. Over the years, I have witnessed many people who simply had given up before a major breakthrough happened. People don't have the patience to see things through. I am not just referring to business, but other things as well, like working out. Look at how many people get excited about getting healthy, and after a month they stop. Just think how many gym memberships are bought when people are excited about getting in shape. Then once they lose the motivation they stop going to the gym. The desired result they looked for will not happen because there wasn't any commitment. If you want things to flourish, you definitely have to commit.

The next two attributes are consistency and persistency. The reason I put these two together is because they go hand-in-hand. I have seen people committed to something but not consistent enough. When doors shut in your face and things are not going your way, will you still remain consistent and persistent to fight for your dreams? This is where the rubber meets the road. People often get commitment and consistency confused. You can be committed to change your eating habits and buy healthy foods for your pantry but only eat healthy sometimes instead of daily.

When I decided to work out in prison I was first committed. Then I consistently showed up even when I didn't want to. I noticed we are consistent in taking care of our kids, getting to school, and working a job. The reason is that we know the price we would pay if we were not committed. Building large organizations, I learned to be consistently persistent.

It didn't matter how many challenges I faced. I learned to keep showing up every day with a positive mindset. This was my secret to success. I learned how to outlast everyone else in my industry. You don't have to have the greatest talent when you have consistency and persistency. Again, you need all of these attributes to become successful at a high level. Even if you master being consistent it will still take time, and you will have to be patient with the process.

Always remember to identify your reason "why" in life. This should be your purpose for wanting to do what you are seeking to do in the first place. Once you are clear on your purpose, it will get easier to be consistent.

The next attribute is to have discipline. This is the attribute I have struggled the most with in my own life. I had to learn that "no" is not a bad word. Also, it might mean that you have to give up on a few things you enjoy doing. This part of discipline I have done fairly well with. You will soon figure out that you might have to change your environment and surroundings in order to set yourself up for success. Champions are strategic in what they do as well as what they allow in their lives. Having the right people in your life with the right mindsets is critical.

Have you ever heard that birds of a feather flock together? There is definitely some truth in that old adage. Ask yourself: does your environment add or delete from your goals? It is imperative that you put yourself in a growth environment. In sports we used to say one small cancer could affect an entire team. We have to be disciplined enough to subtract distractions. Only you know what those distractions are. Failure to remove the root issues and dig up those bad seeds will affect you negatively in the long run. Once you improve with this, things will start happening for you in a big way in business and life.

The last attribute is having heart. This means finding the strength to give more even when everything else in your mind is telling you that you have nothing left. Heart looks just like a marathon. Those who win marathons use each one of these traits in a race. You will come to a point where you have done everything you can, your back is against the wall, and you feel like you have nothing left to give. This will be the moment you get through and create new limits you did not think were possible before. This is what having heart looks like. You are showing your all no matter what curveballs life gives you. This is when you truly define success instead of letting it define you. You will start winning in every area of your life.

I am excited just thinking about the success you will have if you really take ownership of this chapter. I would write every trait down all over your house as a constant reminder of the secret formula. Faith, mindset, loyalty, consistency, persistency, commitment, discipline, and heart.

It is ironic that each of these eight traits can lead anyone to success. Eight is the number of a new beginning. That is perfect in this case because we all are looking for new beginnings in certain areas of our life.

The bottom line is everyone can use improvement in their lives. I know these attributes have worked for me, even when I went through the toughest obstacles in my life. Learning these traits will not happen overnight, but once you master them the sky is the limit. Just remember: they will give you an edge over most people who compete with you on a daily basis. This will truly increase your value in the workplace, business, and in life.

Appendix

Excerpts from Trial Transcript

THE COURT: Mr. Behe, this is one of those times when I wish that I had been presiding at the entry of the guilty plea because I have a feeling there's more to the story than I have heard, because in 20 years, I have not had a single prosecution from the bankruptcy trustee. So something is missing. What don't I know?

THE COURT: Mr. Schiller, this procedure is a little unusual, but as you have heard, you've been sitting here, you've heard a lot of background information on Mr. Vaughn, but, importantly, you've heard his representation to the court that this is really a matter of sloppy bookkeeping. And as I've pointed out, I've never seen one of these prosecutions, and I don't want it to appear that Mr. Vaughn was somehow singled out, so I just need a little background.

Made in the USA
Monee, IL
04 November 2026

67380801R00128